Master WordPress Like A Boss

A Beginner's Guide to Planning, Designing, and Creating Your Very Own Unique WordPress Website

DENNIS LONMO

Master WordPress Like A Boss

Dennis Lonmo
Visit my website at www.dennislonmo.com

Printed in the United States of America

First Printing: Sep 2018

ISBN: 9781720090847

WHAT YOU ARE ABOUT TO MASTER

WordPress is a software that enables you, me, and just about anybody to quickly and with little to no budget set up and run our very own websites. It doesn't matter if you've previously written code or not—you don't have to have any experience whatsoever.

The only thing that matters is your passion and willingness to grab all the knowledge available for the taking, in order to build your skills step by step.

My name is Dennis Lonmo, and I am about to take you on a journey that in the end will provide you with all the necessary know-how to create amazing WordPress websites. I am an entrepreneur by trade and have been building websites for clients since 2008. I run my own digital agency as well as teach highly rated online WordPress courses.

This third book in this series will teach you how to plan, design, and create your very own unique WordPress website.

If you've ever wanted to gain a practical, in-depth understanding of WordPress, this book series will teach you everything you need and more.

TARGET AUDIENCE

I n this book you'll learn everything you need to know to plan, design, and create a WordPress website with no coding needed whatsoever.

This is the third book in a series geared towards a complete beginner's education in WordPress software. The first book in the series covers how to install WordPress locally and on a web host. The second is an in-depth explanation of everything you need to know about the WordPress dashboard.

To get the most out of this third installment, you should already have access to the WordPress dashboard, as this book does not cover how to install WordPress itself, but rather how to create a website with it. ☒

If you don't have WordPress installed, you can check out the first book in this series here: http://a.co/d/4eQ4EMm.

DEDICATION

I dedicate this book to the people out there who have supported, motivated, and inspired me over the years.

To my daughter, who always manages to put a smile on my face, no matter what.

To my mom, who raised me to become the man I am today. Thank you!

To my trusted friends. The warm conversations, honest discussions, and understanding you show when I disappear for months at a time focusing on my business and writing books like this one. Thank you for the daily snaps and memes and everything that we've been through over the years. I wouldn't be able to do this without you.

To the haters, the naysayers, and the enemies. You help me keep my chin up and persevere through the hard times. When the world kicks me to the ground, I use your words and behavior as motivation to get back up and keep going until I

reach my goal. None of my achievements would ever be reached without the likes of you in my life.
I dedicate this book to all of you!

Dennis Lonmo

CONTENTS PAGE

What You Are About to Master 1

Target Audience 3

Dedication 4

Contents Page 6

Chapter 1. Understanding WordPress 10

    What is WordPress? 11

    The Most Popular Platform in the World..13

Chapter 2. Introduction to the Dashboard...15

    Pages 20

    Posts..22

    Categories...26

    Tags...29

    Menus 30

    Important Settings..33

General 33

Reading 33

Permalinks 35

Chapter 3. 38

Planning the Website 38

    First Things First: Adding a "Coming Soon" Page 39

    Website Objectives 43

What Pages Do You Need? 44
Creating a Working Prototype..46
Conclusion...49

Chapter 4..51
Design & Features 51
Websites You Like...52
Choosing the Fonts...54
Deciding on Your Color Scheme..59
Features 63
Conclusion...68

Chapter 5. 70
The Themes...70
Free Themes...71
Paid Themes 75
Choosing Your Theme 78
Conclusion 83

Chapter 6...85
The Plug-ins 85
Free vs Paid...86
Must-Have Plug-ins..90
Choosing Your Plug-ins..93
Conclusion...96

Chapter 7...98
Putting it All Together..98
Installing and Activating the Theme..................................99
Installing and Activating the Plug-ins 105
Getting the Features Up and Running 108
Conclusion 109

Chapter 8...111
Let's Create Some Content...111
How to Write Amazing Copy Fast 112

Know Your Audience..112
Structure the Benefits...112
Important Information First 113
People are Lazy..113

Visual Impression 114
Getting Started 115

    How to Get Free Images...116
    Conclusion 118

Chapter 9. 120
Going Live...120

    Website Checklist..121
    Final Tweaks...129
    Ready to Publish!..130

Chapter 10. 132
Your Next Steps 132
About the Author 133
One Last Thing 135
Resources 136

    WordPress 136
    Plug-ins...137
    Themes 139
    Fonts..139
    Color Scheme 140
    Markup...140
    Free Stock Photo 141
    Dennis Lonmo 142
    Other Books by Dennis Lonmo 142

CHAPTER 1. UNDERSTANDING WORDPRESS

WHAT IS WORDPRESS?

Simply put, WordPress is an open-source software you can use to create a beautiful website, blog, or app.

Let's get right to it!
To get to know WordPress a little better, open up your browser, type in "WordPress.org," and hit *Enter*. The description of WordPress should be viewable on your screen now.

WordPress is a website creation tool. It's a platform where you can create websites completely free of charge.

It presents you with an ocean of opportunities, because you can always add to your website with plug-ins, which are a vital part of almost any WordPress website.

THE MOST POPULAR PLATFORM IN THE WORLD

WordPress is the most popular platform in the world. It is used by non-coders as well as pro coders.
You can use it however you like, and you can do really awesome stuff with it, even on
a small budget.

In this book we're going to use WordPress completely for free. Everything you learn here, you can do completely for free—as long as you have an internet connection and a working computer (or any other device that you feel comfortable using).

Let's just dive into it, shall we?

CHAPTER 2.
INTRODUCTION TO THE
DASHBOARD

Let's talk about the WordPress dashboard.

Once you've logged in and you visit the WordPress dashboard, the first thing you notice is the dashboard homepage. Right now it consists of Gutenberg, the "Welcome to WordPress" widget, and on the middle of the page, you have four boxes lined up. These boxes are: "at a glance," "quick draft," "activity," and "WordPress events and news."

Take a moment to check these out.

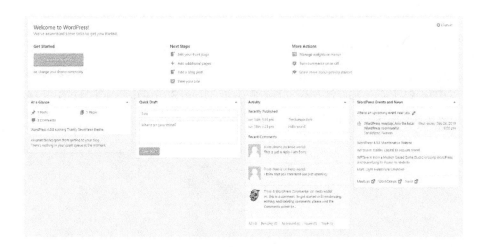

On the top of the page, you have a top bar, which consists of the WordPress logo on the left and the option to visit your site. You also have the options to upgrade your theme, check your comments, and add a new post, media, page, or user.

On the right side of this page, you have the options to edit your profile and log out; on the left side, you have a menu which points you to your home, posts, media, pages, comments, appearance, plug-ins, users, tools, settings, and the option to collapse the menu.

Depending on your hosting provider, this menu could be set up differently. A lot of hosting providers add their own plug-ins when you create a WordPress installation using their servers.

But the standard WordPress navigation menu, without any additional plug-ins, directs you to the dashboard, posts, media, pages, comments, appearance, plug-ins, users, tools, settings, and the option to collapse the list at the bottom. So we're going to go through the posts, pages, and menus, and we'll also try tweaking some settings.

Why go through these few specific options?

Because these are basically what you need to set up your WordPress site correctly. At the most elementary level, you just need to know how to add pages, posts, and menus and how to tweak the settings to fit your needs.

PAGES

To see your site's pages, go to the dashboard, where you see "Pages" between "Media" and "Comments." Click on that. And there you have it.

So now we can click on "Add New." The options that you have are to publish the page, save a draft, preview, edit status, change its visibility, and publish immediately.

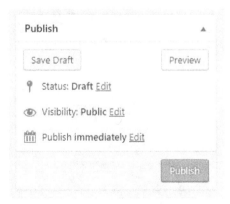

You can set a parent page, order the page, and add a featured image if you wish.

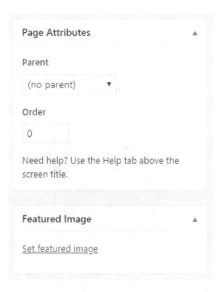

You can also enter a page title, add your text, upload a featured image, and click "publish." So, that's really it!

As you'll see in the following section, we have a lot more options available for posts than we do for pages.

POSTS

To view your posts, click on "Posts" on the left side of the screen, underneath "Dashboard" in the navigation menu.

You'll see options to view all your posts, add new ones, and view the categories and tags. We're going to concentrate on "All Posts" right now.

If you click on "All Posts," you'll be directed to a page where you can add a new post, search your posts, do some bulk actions, and filter them by date and category.

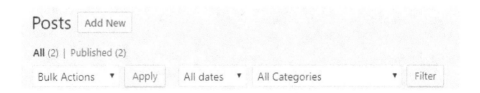

What we're going to do now is add a new post, so you can learn how that's done. First off, click "Add New," which will take you to a new page where you can write, design, and publish news, articles, tutorials, and anything else you may desire.

You will see fields available to enter your title and text.

On the right-hand side of the page, you can save your post as a draft, update status and visibility, and publish.

The different formats (another option available on the right-hand side) are something that you really don't need to worry about when you're starting out. Just keep it in a standard format.

Format   ▲

- ◉ 📌 Standard
- ○ 📝 Aside
- ○ 🖼 Image
- ○ ▶ Video
- ○ ❝ Quote
- ○ 🔗 Link
- ○ 🖼 Gallery
- ○ 🎵 Audio

Underneath, you have categories and tags options, and you can set a featured image for the post.

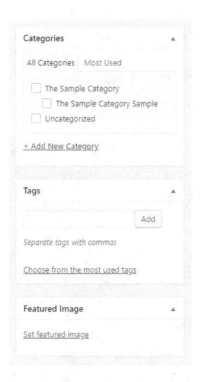

Play around on this page. Once you've entered a title and text into the corresponding fields, assigned the post to a category, and added your featured image, you can just click on "Publish," and you'll have your new post up and running.

CATEGORIES

Let's check out the categories in the WordPress dashboard. To start, click on "Categories" in the submenu to "Posts."

This categorization tool helps you organize your posts in whichever ways are most useful to you.

Say you have a company that deals with digital marketing; within digital marketing, you have AdWords, Facebook, email marketing, and so on.

Categories

Add New Category

Name

The name is how it appears on your site.

Slug

The "slug" is the URL-friendly version of the name. It is usually all lowercase and contains only letters, numbers, and hyphens.

Parent Category

None

Categories, unlike tags, can have a hierarchy. You might have a Jazz category, and under that have children categories for Bebop and Big Band. Totally optional.

Description

The description is not prominent by default; however, some themes may show it.

Add New Category

Bulk Actions ▾ Apply

Name

The Sample Category

— The Sample Category Sample

Uncategorized

Name

Bulk Actions ▾ Apply

Note:
Deleting a category does not delete the posts in
Categories can be selectively converted to tags

You can add a category called "Marketing" and then create a subcategory called "Facebook" and another called "AdWords" underneath it. Those two categories would then have "Marketing" as their parent category.

Underneath you see the category slug. The slug will automatically be created as your posts' category name if you don't manually enter one in that field.

Slug

The "slug" is the URL-friendly version of the name. It is usually all lowercase and contains only letters, numbers, and hyphens.

Parent Category

None ▾

Categories, unlike tags, can have a hierarchy. You might have a Jazz category, and under that have children categories for Bebop and Big Band. Totally optional.

You then have the option to select a parent category from the drop-down menu underneath "Slug" if you wish. So if you've already created a category for "Digital Marketing," you can easily add your new category to that parent category.

At the bottom of the right-hand side panel, you have the description field. Most WordPress themes won't display the category description anywhere other than in the WordPress dashboard.

Description

The description is not prominent by default; however, some themes may show it.

Add New Category

Note, however, that when you're just starting out, it's not necessary to spend time on this category description.

Once you've entered information in the fields that we have walked through at this point, click on "Add New Category," and there you are—a new category ready to go.

TAGS

Click on "Tags" located under "Categories" in the navigation menu.
There you have the option to add a new tag. Since the process to do so is basically the same as with categories, we won't walk through each step of adding and editing them.

The only real difference is that you don't have the option to add a parent tag, as you can with categories.

Tags

Add New Tag

Name

The name is how it appears on your site.

Slug

The "slug" is the URL-friendly version of the name. It is usually all lowercase and contains only letters, numbers, and hyphens.

Description

The description is not prominent by default; however, some themes may show it.

Add New Tag

MENUS

To get to "Menus," go over to the left-side navigation menu and hover over "Appearance." In the submenu that comes up, you'll see "Menus." Click.

Here you have the Menus page. To create a new menu, just click on "create a new menu" up on the right, under the "Edit Menus" tab.

That will take you to a new page which doesn't contain anything (because we don't have a menu yet).

To create one, we just enter a name for the new menu in the "Menu Name" field and then click "Create Menu."
We now have a new menu!

As you see in the screenshot, you have some boxes on the left-hand side. These boxes help you add content to your new menu.
Click on one of them to open it and see the content.

Once you've added some posts, pages, and any other content to your website, you'll have a lot to add to your menu.

Let's say you have created four pages and now you want to add them to a menu. Go to the "Create Menu" page ("Dashboard → Appearance → Menus"), choose the pages you would like to add to a new menu, and save it.

The pages will now be visible in your new menu.

IMPORTANT SETTINGS

To visit the settings, go to "Dashboard →Settings." Click on that, and some options will appear underneath it: general, writing, reading, discussion, media, permalink, and privacy.

General

We'll start with the general settings. On this page you'll see the site title and the tagline, which you can change to whatever you want for your site.

You have a lot of options here to make other changes as well, but as you're just starting out, you don't need to bother with those now. Come back to tweak them later.

Reading

Next, check out "Reading," which is by far the most important part of setting up and maintaining your site: from here you can manage your homepage, blog, and search engine visibility settings.

Most of the time, your default WordPress installation will have your homepage set to display your latest posts. If you are going to create a business site or anything other than a pure blog, I recommend that you create a new page (call it "Front Page") and set this to "a static page."

This way, you have one established page which welcomes all visitors to your site.

Reading Settings

Your homepage displays

- Your latest posts
- A static page (select below)

Homepage: Home Page ▾

Posts page: Blog ▾

Remember to uncheck the "Search Engine Visibility" checkbox and click "Save Changes."

Search Engine Visibility

☐ Discourage search engines from indexing this site

It is up to search engines to honor this request.

Save Changes

Permalinks

The third thing that we're going to check out in these settings is the permalinks.
On most websites, you'll see a permalink that looks something like this: "yourdomain.com/your-blog-post/." This is known as the "post name" structure.

In a new WordPress installation, however, this is often set to "Plain." This will make your permalink look something like this to your visitors: "yourdomain.com/?p=180."

Instead of showing the post or page name (which is preferable), it displays the ID number of the page that you're on.

So if your permalink structure is set to "Plain," change it to "Post name" instead.

Now that you have a basic understanding of the dashboard, I advise you to play around and familiarize yourself with it a little bit.

In the next chapter, we'll start to plan out our website.

CHAPTER 3.
PLANNING THE WEBSITE

I n this chapter we will start to plan out our websites. Some of you may think that this is a waste of time, and just want to get going to create the site right away. But I promise you that by planning out your site *before* you start creating content, you'll save yourself a ton of time and frustration.

When we plan the site out, we avoid having to go back and forth all the time, adding and deleting plug-ins and themes, spending money on things we do not need, and so on.

You're about to learn how to effectively plan your site from start to finish so that when you are ready to start creating it, you'll know exactly what to do to get it up and running in no time.

FIRST THINGS FIRST: ADDING A "COMING SOON" PAGE

Before you do anything else with your site, you need to add a "Coming Soon" page. What this does is protect your site *while* you're creating it. If somebody tries to access it, they'll be met with a page that looks something like this.

This Site is Coming Soon
I hope You're Ready

The simplest way to make a "Coming Soon" page is to add a new plug-in.

Go to "Dashboard → Plug-ins → Add New" and search for "Coming Soon" in the search field. You'll get some results looking something like this:

The one you want is "Coming Soon Page and Maintenance Mode by SeedProd," so just click "Install Now" and activate it right away.

You'll be directed to the plug-in settings, where you can see that the "Coming Soon" mode has not been automatically enabled. To get it working the way you need it to, click on "Enable Coming Soon Mode" and save the changes.

If you want to brand the "Coming Soon" page, you see that you have the options to upload your logo and add a personalized headline and a message.
I recommend that you at least add a headline and some text. It could be as simple as: "This page is coming soon" (as a headline) and "I hope you're ready" (as a message).

When you're done, click "Save Changes" and open up your website in a new incognito window (or just log out of the dashboard) and see if your "Coming Soon" page works as intended.

This Site is Coming Soon
I hope You're Ready

If it works, anybody who tries to visit your site will be met by this page. Only authorized users who are logged in can actually look at the website.

WEBSITE OBJECTIVES

Before you start to really build the site, you need to plan it out. Again, why? Well, by planning out your website before you start to build it, you know what you are building *while* you build it. And believe me, that's a huge timesaver.

There are a couple of things you should think about during the planning phase. The first thing is the objective of the site. Here are a few common examples of objectives:

- Drive Traffic
- Generate Leads
- Generate Sales
- Increase Awareness
- Customer Support
- Branding

I recommend that you take a few minutes and write down some of your goals for this site. Ask yourself *why* you are creating it.

WHAT PAGES DO YOU NEED?

When it comes to creating pages for a new website, the golden rule is that every business is unique, and therefore every website has different needs.

With that said, your website will have visitors (hopefully), and those visitors have certain expectations that you as a business and website owner should strive to meet.

A good thing to keep in mind when deciding which pages your website should have is that *people do business with other people—not websites.* So even though a website is one of the most accessible ways to introduce yourself to the world, people want to get to know you, your employees, and your company on a personal level.

With that said, here are eight pages you should think about adding to your website.

1. Homepage
2. About Page
3. Services Page
4. Testimonials Page
5. Terms and Conditions Page
6. Privacy Policy Page
7. Blog Page
8. Contact Page

So, write down the pages you want your website to have. Remember, you can add and remove pages whenever you want later, but you should add some pages before you make the website available.

The better you plan out your website, the easier it will be to set up.

CREATING A WORKING PROTOTYPE

A working prototype is basically just a website that hasn't been designed yet, but that has working menus with working pages so that you can look at it and make your final decision on the choices you made regarding the site structure.

To accomplish this, go to Pages →Add New and start adding the pages that you decided on in the previous step.

This is just to show you how to get a prototype up and running. The pages I've added in these screenshots could be completely different from what you want, so just look at what I am doing as an example.

Once you've added all your pages, go to "Appearance →Menus" and add the pages to the menu that we created in Chapter 2.

With that task done, let's give the menu a location. Look for that option at the bottom of your screen (see "Display Location" at the bottom of the screenshot above).

Check the location you want the menu to appear and then click "Save Menu."
Now you can check out your prototype.
Go to the top bar, hover over the site name, and click on "Visit Site."

There you have your new menu!

Click on it to check that the pages are working and its structure is how you intended it to be.

Be sure to test every menu item (page) to make sure that it works as desired and that it has the correct parent page (if you gave it one).

To check the parent page, take a look at the URL: If the page that you're on has a parent page, it will display the parent page name before the current page name in the permalink. See the example below:

"YOURWEBSITE.COM/ABOUT/PRODUCTS"

If everything is in order, you now have a working prototype!

CONCLUSION

Congratulations on reaching the end of the planning chapter!

By now, you have decided on what pages to use, created a visual sitemap, and have a working prototype to design your website around.

In the next chapter we will go over color schemes, fonts, and the kinds of features you may want.

DENNIS LONMO

CHAPTER 4.
DESIGN & FEATURES

N ow we will dive in to the design and features aspect of the website.

You'll learn how to decide your website's color scheme and font, how to get inspiration from other websites you like, and what kind of features you want your website to have.

WEBSITES YOU LIKE

The very first thing you need to do to figure out your perfect design is to think about four websites you like when it comes to *design*.

So take a pause and write down your top four websites before you continue reading.

To narrow down your favorites from four to two, you have to reflect on what you really like about each one. Then eliminate whichever two you like the least. Use your gut feeling and look at the colors and elements the websites display.

The top two websites you're left with is what you are going to base your design on. Just to be clear, you are not copying them, but they will be your main inspiration to get going with your own design.

This step is really important because in the next sections you will use this information to nail down your fonts and color scheme. So, spend some time with this. No need to rush.

CHOOSING THE FONTS

To make your website truly unique to you, you should add some custom fonts.

There are a *lot* of themes out there that come loaded with hundreds of custom fonts.

You want to avoid those, however, because they can slow your site down considerably. They'll slow you down because they have to load hundreds of unused fonts, even though you just use a couple of them.

AaBbCcDdEeFfGgHhIi
JjKkLlMmNnOoPpQq
RrSsTtUuVvWwXxYyZz

You are going to learn how to add custom fonts properly, without affecting your site's performance in any noticeable way.

First of all, you need to find the fonts you want to use.

To do that, you can check out Google Fonts (https://fonts.google.com/), FontSquirrel (https://www.fontsquirrel.com/), and Fonts.com (https://www.fonts.com/).

Get a sense of which fonts you like.

It can be difficult to decide which one to use. But you need not fear—there is a very nice tool out there to help you with that.

Search for the site "Font Pair" (https://fontpair.co/) in your open browser.

Featured Font Pairs

At the top of the page, you can click on different types of font "families" and find a combination that you like by scrolling down to view them.

When you decide on a font pair, you are ready to install them. Remember that too many fonts will slow down your site considerably, so just install two fonts to use on your website.

Now, let's get these fonts installed. To do that, visit your WordPress dashboard, go to "Plug-ins → Add New" and search for the Easy Google Fonts plug-in (https://wordpress.org/plugins/easy-google-fonts/).

Click "Install" and activate it right away.
Now that you have activated it, you can open the customizer and click "Typography" in the customizer menu.

Now you see the different parts of your website where you can apply the new fonts. You also have lots of other options here—you can change style, padding, size, margins, and more.

These options vary depending on the theme that you are using right now. In the screenshot above, I'm using a 2018 theme.

Now choose the fonts you'd like to use and click "Publish" to see how it looks on the site.

THIS IS THE SUBTITLE

It is a long established fact that a reader will be distracted by the readable content of a page when looking at its layout. The point of using **Lorem Ipsum** is that it has a more-or-less normal distribution of letters, as opposed to using 'Content here, content here', making it look like readable English.

Great! You've now added custom fonts to your website!

DECIDING ON YOUR COLOR SCHEME

Choosing the right color scheme for your website is essential. Not only does it determine how your site looks, but it can even be an important tool for you to generate more sales, conversions, and more. But finding the right color scheme doesn't have to be difficult at all.

The first thing you need to do is choose the primary color for your site. To do this, revisit the top two websites you wrote down earlier.

Look at the colors they implement and determine whether those colors are something you would want on your site.

When you have decided on the colors, visit https://coolors.co/.

The super fast color schemes generator!

Create, save and share perfect palettes in seconds!

Start the Generator, it's free!

Coolors is a color scheme generator. It's very easy to use—simply hit the space bar to generate a new color scheme. You can modify a color manually and lock it down. You can also download color schemes to use in your projects later.

So, let's say you want to use blue as your primary color. Browse the schemes that Coolors generates with this color.

You don't have to be a world-class designer to accomplish a great-looking color scheme.

On the next page, you see an infographic that tells you a little about the psychology of colors and the emotions which popular colors invoke in us.

THE PSYCHOLOGY OF COLOR

YELLOW

Creativity

Optimism   **Happiness**   **Positive Energy**

GREEN

Renewal

Growth   Soothing   Reassurance

BLUE

Strength

Intellectual   Refreshing   Trust

RED

Power

Passion   Danger   Attention

DENNIS LONMO

DENNIS LONMO

FEATURES

Now that you have the fonts and color scheme nailed down, you can look at the features you want on your site. To get started,

I'll walk you through ten of the most popular features you see in modern WordPress websites today.

1. Contact Form

This is the form you usually see on the "Contact" page, which enables you to contact the site owners or support directly from the site.

2. Analytics

"Analytics" is the statistics of your site's traffic and visitor behavior. It could be extremely powerful if you spend some time looking at it, because you'll learn what your visitors are doing at your site, which pages they're spending time on, and which they immediately bounce off of.

3. Conversion Optimization

This is how you get new subscribers, sales, email subscribers, and so on. You have probably been at a website where you've experienced some kind of pop-up that wants you to subscribe or buy something on their site. That is conversion optimization.

4. Backup

Let's say your site gets hacked or you manage to mess it up in some way or another. Having a backup software run continual backups for you will give you the option to roll back yesterday's backup and set everything back in place as it should be. If you don't have any backup options, your website is very vulnerable.

5. SEO

Search engine optimization is a factor that helps you rank in the search engines so that you can get more traffic to your site.

6. Email Marketing Automation

You've most likely heard of MailChimp, the email marketing automation platform. It helps you connect with your subscribers via email and also has plenty of useful tools, like automation.

7. CDN

CDN, or content delivery network, is a helpful way to speed up and secure your site. The way it works is by hiding your real IP. It sends all traffic to data centers elsewhere on the globe and serves your website from the data center that's nearest to the location that each visitor is browsing from. Cloudflare is a well-known CDN.

8. Gallery

You probably know what a gallery is, and yes, themes usually have a built-in function that allows you to create galleries. But the problem is that most of the time, those galleries are pretty general. They're boring and not very amazing to look at. To achieve great-looking galleries, use plug-ins like Envira.

9. Page Builder

Most of the popular premium themes out there come with a page builder. A page builder is exactly what it sounds like: a software that helps you build pages, with a drag-and-drop functionality. It can be beneficial or it can be a nightmare, depending on which one you choose. In my humble opinion, the best page builder out there is the Beaver Builder plug-in.

10. Social Shares

You've probably seen some social icons that you can click on to share articles you're reading online. They can come in a range of color and designs. No matter what, you should have something like this installed if you are going to blog on your website. I don't have a number-one recommendation here, as there are a lot of good options. Figure out which one you like best and suits your site. Try searching for social shares in the WordPress Plug-in repository to check some of them out.

Now that you have an overview of some of the most popular features on websites today, you can write down all the ones you would like your own website to have.

If you spend some time with these now, you will save a ton of time when you get to the chapter where you'll be adding the features to your website.

CONCLUSION

Congratulations on reaching it to the end of the design and features chapter!

BY now you have nailed down the color scheme and fonts you want on your website, and you also know what features you want your website to have.

In the next chapter you'll get to know WordPress themes— what they really are and how you choose the best one for your website.

CHAPTER 5.
THE THEMES

We've now covered website objectives, prototypes, color schemes, fonts, and features. We are done with the planning phase; now is the time to take a look at some WordPress themes.

In this chapter you'll learn the difference between free and paid themes, and how you can use the information you have learned thus far to choose the perfect theme for your site.

FREE THEMES

If you go to "Dashboard → Appearance → Themes → Add New," you will get to a page that shows you a lot of free themes that you can install and activate with just a few clicks.

You can search for themes with keywords related to your business up in the right corner. You can also sort them by popularity, features, and so on.

But why are the themes that you see here free? What is the difference between the free and the paid themes?

Well, there are a couple of things to consider if you are pondering using a completely free theme.

- **Free themes are often poorly supported**

This means that if something goes wrong, you have to buy an upgrade or license to get help from the developer.

- **They have fewer features than paid themes**

"You get what you pay for" is an expression that applies nicely here. Free themes are very often put out there in order to entice you to buy the paid theme as an upgrade.
It's like the people offering free samples in the supermarket—they're not doing it to be nice; they want you to buy the product. WordPress gives out a free version of a theme which only contains a fraction of the features that the premium version of that theme offers.

- **They could be abandoned**

Websites needs care and love to stay healthy and up to date. But without any money coming in, developers often abandon their free themes to start work on something else.

This results in outdated themes with security risks and other potential errors.

With that said, it probably seems like I'm against free themes. I'm not. I think they're a perfect option for people getting started with WordPress. So here are some pros:

- **Free themes are free**

They don't cost you anything.

- **They install quickly**

If you install a free theme from the WordPress dashboard, you'll have that theme installed and activated within two minutes maximum.

- **It's a great way to get started!**

If you put the two previous pros together, you get a quick and great way to get started and to gain experience with WordPress.

Whether or not you want to check out free themes is entirely up to you. A lot of people use them to great success.

Just be wary of the cons I listed above, and do your due diligence before installing and activating your new theme.

PAID THEMES

There are lots of advantages with premium themes. But where do you find them? Where is the best place to purchase high quality and amazing themes?

We'll take a look into that right now.
Visit https://themeforest.net/category/wordpress. ThemeForest is a website where you can buy premium themes at great prices. Developers put their themes up for sale here–in essence, it's a marketplace for themes.

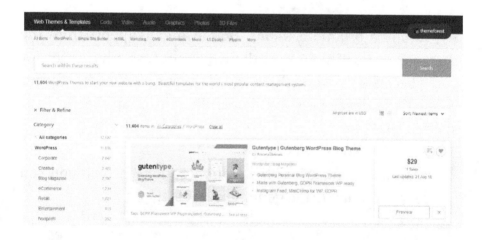

If you click on WordPress on the gray bar underneath the header, you can browse categories, tags, prices, dates added, and much more—and then you can use the search bar to specify your search even further.

You have a great chance of finding a theme that fits your specs and niche.

But why buy a theme when you can get one for free with just a few clicks in your WordPress dashboard?

Well, the most significant advantage premium themes have, as I hinted in the previous section, is features.
There are a lot of themes from different developers being published all the time on ThemeForest, which makes the marketplace competitive, and as a result of that competitive spirit, themes are usually jam-packed with features and included plug-ins.

If you buy a premium theme, you also get support from the theme authors. This makes the whole process a lot easier for you—because if something goes wrong, you can always contact the developers and hopefully get an answer to your specific problem.

You also have tons of customization options, which you can use to make your theme genuinely unique.

There are some cons to think about before purchasing a premium theme, however:

- The site can be slow, heavy, and poorly coded, which is bad for SEO and your visitors.

- The site may have *too many* features, which makes it very vulnerable to conflicts if you try to install new plug-ins, for example. To have ten features available and only use two of them is not a good idea when it comes to WordPress themes.

CHOOSING YOUR THEME

Now you know the difference between free and paid themes and what you need to look out for in both types. But how do you decide which to use?

To make the selection process a lot easier, I'll give you six factors to take into consideration when choosing the best theme for your website.

- **Responsive**

Gone are the days when the responsive site was a forward-thinking idea that was considered a feature of the best themes out there.

Today, responsiveness is completely normal—as it should be. Visitors, search engines, and WordPress itself expects your theme to be mobile-friendly and responsive to any device.

- **Great Documentation**

The theme you decide to go with, whether it's free or paid, should have excellent documentation and support.

You'll probably experience some hiccups along the way, and without detailed documentation or support, you'll waste a lot of valuable time fixing minor problems—time you could be using to grow your traffic and audience.

- **Watch the Page Builder**

Nowadays, a lot of the popular premium themes out there come with in-built page builders. I briefly talked about page builders before—I love great page builders.

But a problem occurs when you buy a theme, build every page on your website with a page builder, and then decide to switch your theme.

If the new theme uses a different page builder (or maybe none whatsoever), you'll be spending days or even weeks cleaning up all the pages you created with the previous builder.

If you are going to use a page builder, make sure to use a popular one that you can purchase externally and is not built into the theme itself.

You'll find my top recommendation in the chapter on features.

- **SEO Optimized**

"SEO optimized" is probably the wrong term to use, but "SEO friendly," at the very least, should be a top priority when choosing a new theme.

For someone with little to zero knowledge of SEO, it can be challenging to check out this issue on your own.

A tip: Use the W3C Markup Validation Tool (https://validator.w3.org/) and check the comments on the theme that you are purchasing to see what other buyers have to say about it.

- **Ratings And Reviews**

This is the main tip I have for you, and probably the most obvious one.

Always check the ratings and reviews of a theme you're considering purchasing.
If the theme consistently gets poor ratings, look for something else.

- **Plug-ins**

Maybe there are some specific plug-ins you already know that you want to use. If that's the case, check the documentation or ask the developer if the theme supports that plug-in.
Most themes these days have support for the popular and well-known plug-ins out there.

But always make sure that the theme you want to install, whether free or paid, supports the plug-ins you need to build the website you want.

If you don't do this, you could end up spending a lot of time fixing issues on your site because of poor plug-in support.

- **The Feature Trap**

Don't fall in the feature trap. What I mean by that is that we all tend to think "more is better." When it comes to WordPress themes, that is not the case at all.

Look for themes that have the features you want and need, not the themes that have *everything*. Those extras will only slow your site down and be a nightmare to maintain.

The chance of finding a theme that has just the features you need and nothing else is slim to none. But there is a huge difference between a theme that is lacking a few or has a few extra and a theme that has twenty features, of which you only need four.

Simplicity is something to always keep in mind when choosing your theme. With the tips above, you should be ready to pick your theme and get one step further in creating your fantastic website.

CONCLUSION

Congratulations on making it to the end of the themes chapter. You now know everything you need in order to create an amazing website in no time. But wait, there is something missing, and it's one of the most crucial parts of any WordPress website: the plug-ins.

In the next chapter we will cover everything you need to know about plug-ins—which ones you have to install, who you should choose, and the difference between free and paid ones.

CHAPTER 6.
THE PLUG-INS

We've now done the planning and you have decided on the theme you want to use.
There is just one tiny thing missing: plug-ins.

In this chapter you'll learn the difference between free and paid plug-ins and how you can use the information you have so far to choose the right plug-ins for your site's features.

FREE VS PAID

First off, we will start with what a plug-in is. A plug-in is an app that you can add to your WordPress theme in order to introduce new features.

It works kind of like your smartphone: you install an app, and you have a new feature on the phone. It's not complicated at all.

Now, let's talk about the differences you can experience when choosing a paid or a free plug-in.

Go to the WordPress dashboard and click "Appearance → Plug-ins → Add New." You will get a new page that shows you free plug-ins that you can install and activate with just a few clicks.

You can also search for plug-ins and sort them by popularity, features, and so on.

But why are the plug-ins free? What are the differences between free and paid plug-ins?

The answer to that question is almost the same as with themes (see the previous chapter), so I'll go through them quickly.

Free Plug-ins

Cons:

- They have fewer features.

- A stand-alone plug-in with no upgrade option has a real danger of being abandoned, and it probably doesn't have great documentation or support.

- Because of the danger of abandonment by the developer, free plug-ins can pose a real security risk.

Pros:

- They are completely free.

- You can test them out before you buy a premium version.

- You can install and activate them right away, without having to register an account anywhere.

So why do we need to pay for a plug-in?

Premium Plug-ins

Pros:

- More features

- Complete plug-in

- Premium support

- Customization options

Cons:
- Offer a lot of features you don't need

- Weigh your site down

- Expensive (they often cost the same if not more than a full-blown premium theme)

I mentioned most of these pros and cons in greater detail in the themes chapter, so feel free to go back and check them out.

However, what you see here is a great summarization of free and paid plug-ins.

MUST-HAVE PLUG-INS

Installing the right plug-ins can make or break your website. It can send you down the path of peace and success or the path of errors and frustration.

Below you see the three types of plug-ins I recommend no matter what kind of WordPress website you have.

1. Sucuri/WordFence

Sucuri and WordFence are two different plug-ins, but they serve the same function for your website.

They protect it from external and internal threats. What I mean by that is that they run security scans, block pending attacks, notify you if something is going wrong, and give you detailed reports of what's going on your site.

Check them both out and choose the one you like the most.

2. Yoast SEO

Yoast is a fantastic plug-in that lets you monitor your posts and pages regarding SEO status.
It has a straightforward interface that allows you to quickly create metadata when you add new posts or pages.

The plug-in gives you tips and tricks on how to improve your content, notifies you if something important is missing, or if you have a conflict anywhere on your site when it comes to SEO.

3. MonsterInsights

MonsterInsights let you track visitors and move your whole analytics dashboard straight into your WordPress dashboard.

This way, you have this information all in one place and you can quickly check up on how your sites are doing traffic-wise and how your visitors are engaging with your website.

Remember to check these plug-ins out and see what you think about them.
In my opinion, these are the three must-have plug-ins that every website needs when it goes live.

CHOOSING YOUR PLUG-INS

Now that you have all your features nailed down, you need to find the plug-ins that best suit them.

To accomplish that, you have two options: You can go to "Dashboard → Plug-ins → Add New" and search for plug-ins there, or you can use Google.

The WordPress search function isn't the best for the search you need to perform, because first of all, you need to find plug-ins that have the features you need, and then after that, you need to decide on which you want to use.

Check your notes from the earlier chapters and see what kind of features you wanted your website to have. To find plug-ins that match them, search for the feature first on Google, and then on WordPress.

In the Google search bar, write "email marketing WordPress plug-in," and you should find a lot of useful plug-ins.

If you do not want to spend time searching for a plug-in that fits your specific needs, I have recommended one plug-in for each of the features I listed in the design and features chapter.

Feature		Plug-in	
☐	Contact Forms	☑	Contact Form 7
☐	Analytics	☑	MonsterInsights
☐	Conversion Optimization	☑	OptinMonster
☐	Backup	☑	UpdraftPlus
☐	SEO	☑	Yoast SEO
☐	Email Marketing Automation	☑	MailChimp
☐	Gallery	☑	Envira Gallery
☐	CDN	☑	Cloudflare
☐	Page Builder	☑	Beaver Builder
☐	Social Shares	☑	Ultimate Social Media Icons

Check them out and decide what works best for you.

CONCLUSION

Congratulations on reaching the end of the plug-ins chapter. You now have everything you need to create a website. It's all planned out and ready to go!

In the next chapter, you will use this information to create a beautiful and functional WordPress website. Because you have laid the groundwork, this will be a fun process that will take you a very short amount of time (compared to if you were to just dive right into it without planning or doing any work up front).

So, gather all the information from the previous chapters, and get ready for some awesome website creation!

CHAPTER 7.
PUTTING IT ALL
TOGETHER

N ow that you have done all the work up front, the creation process will lack all the time and frustration it would otherwise entail.

You already know and have everything you need to make it happen.
In this chapter, you'll put all that knowledge into action.

INSTALLING AND ACTIVATING THE THEME

Bring out your notes to remind yourself which theme you decided on (if you don't have a theme yet, go back and visit that chapter and then choose a theme so that you can follow along while we install and activate it).

Depending on what kind of theme you chose, you can either install it directly through the WordPress dashboard just by browsing the theme repository.

Let's say you decided to go with a premium theme from ThemeForest. The first thing we need to do is to download it.

So head over to the downloads page and download the theme files.

When you do so, you have the option to download only the theme files, only the license code, or both; choose both so that you get everything you need in one go and don't have to backtrack and download the rest later.

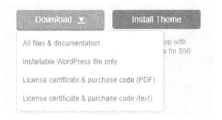

You see now that a zip file has been created.

themeforest-your-theme-2018

The first thing to do is to unzip the main file. When you open the unzipped folder, you will see a new folder that is zipped—DON'T UNZIP THIS. This is the folder we will upload to our WordPress site.

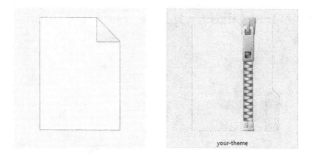

To upload it, go to "Dashboard → Appearance → Themes → Add New," find your theme, and click "Upload."

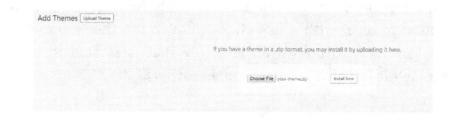

Then you can install and activate it right away.

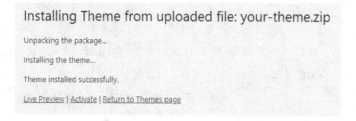

You now have installed and activated your new theme, but it doesn't look like the theme you saw in the demo, does it?

To make it look like that, we need to import the demo content.

WEBSITE   THEME DEMO

This can be done in various ways, but usually, you get an option to do it with a few clicks right in the theme options. Or, you have to upload an XML file that is located in your theme files (which we downloaded earlier).

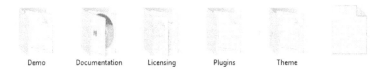

Demo   Documentation   Licensing   Plugins   Theme

However, before that, we need to install and activate the required plug-ins.

Most premium themes come with the plug-ins that are necessary for the theme to function correctly. If that's the case for your theme, you'll probably see a notification at the top of your dashboard (or you will see information about it in the theme documentation).

This theme requires the following plugins: *Your Theme Addons*, *Your Theme Demo Importer*, *Newsletter*, *Redux Framework* and *Visual Composer*.
This theme recommends the following plugins: *Contact Form 7*, *Convert Plug*, *Woocommerce* and *Yellow Pencil*.
Begin installing plugins | Dismiss this notice

If you need to use the XML file that comes with the theme, you'll get clear instructions on how to do that on the theme's "Welcome" page or in the theme documentation. It can vary from theme to theme, so I recommend you look through the documentation before you continue to see if that's something that's necessary for your chosen theme.

In this theme, I can import it right here on the "Theme Options" page. I'll click on that.

Demo Importer

Importing a demo will create pages, posts, add images, theme options, widgets and others. IMPORTANT: Please activate all the required plugins before importing demo content.

Demo Content

This may take a while, depending on the content you are importing, so just be patient.

When it's done, visit the front page of your site and see how it looks. If it looks like the demo you saw before you bought the theme, then you're good to go!

INSTALLING AND ACTIVATING THE PLUG-INS

The next step now is to install the plug-ins which you have already figured out that you need in order to make your site work the way you want it to.

The first thing is to install the "must-have" plug-ins we talked about earlier in the book. If you don't remember them at the moment, check your notes (or go back to the chapter on plug-ins).

Let's install the MonsterInsights plug-in right now, so that you can learn the process and easily install and activate the rest of your plug-ins.

Go to "Dashboard → Plug-ins → Add New" and then search for "MonsterInsights." Your results should look like this:

When you click on the "MonsterInsights" plug-in, you will get a modal showing this:

Click on the button that says "Install Now," and when it's done, click on "Activate."

As you see in the screenshot below, you'll be directed straight to the plug-ins settings page.

Here you can tweak the plug-in settings to fit your needs.

At this point, 99% of the time, you'll be prompted to buy a premium version of the plug-in, but that's usually not necessary. By all means do so if it will give you some features you want to have on your site, however.

And that's really it! You've successfully installed and activated your first plug-in. Wasn't that easy?

Just follow the same steps with the other plug-ins you need, and you'll have your desired features up and running in no time!

GETTING THE FEATURES UP AND RUNNING

If you found a theme that does everything you need it to, you don't need to install any more plug-ins than those you already have. However, if you still want some additional features, follow the same process as you did with MonsterInsights.

The only difference that may arise in the process is once the new plug-in is activated and you need to set it up. That's where the importance of good documentation and excellent support comes into play.

There are tens of thousands of plug-ins out there, and they all have different "Settings" pages on the dashboard.

The premium and popular plug-ins tend to have great step-by-step guides once you've installed them, so follow their instructions and you'll have everything up and running in no time!

CONCLUSION

Congratulations on putting it all together! You now have a fully functioning and fantastic website.

However, we are not quite ready to push it live yet—we need some content, and in the next section, we will cover exactly that topic.

CHAPTER 8.
LET'S CREATE SOME CONTENT

We are nearing the finish line, and I congratulate you for accomplishing so much in a short amount of time.

In this chapter, you will give your website some much-needed content.

You'll learn how to write excellent website copy quickly and how you can get your hands on high-quality images you can use on your website entirely for free.

HOW TO WRITE AMAZING COPY FAST

The first thing we need to clarify before we dig into the actual tips and methods is that absolutely everybody can write great web copy!

There are proven methods and simple steps to follow in order to write copy that engages, impresses, and converts.

So with that out the way, let's get started on how you can create your fantastic web copy, fast.

Know Your Audience

Understand exactly who you're writing for and what makes them tick. Answer the questions they may ask themselves when checking out your website.

Finding your audience and figuring out who they are involves everything from demographics to age and gender. Before you write a single sentence, figure out your visitor base.

Structure the Benefits

Give your readers a reason why they should choose you and your business.

Don't just give a bulleted list; describe what pains and/or problems the reader will solve or avoid by using your products or services.

Important Information First

Whenever a visitor lands on your website, it is more than likely because they are looking for something and came across your website in the process.

That's why it's extremely important to give them the information they seek as soon as possible.

Think about it. If you wanted to find a refrigerator to buy online, and you clicked on a search result in Google that took you to a site that sells refrigerators, the first things you would want to see are the price, supplier, and photos of the refrigerator.

The more time it took you to find that information, the less likely you would be to buy from that website.

People are Lazy

We want what's easy to get, we want it fast, and we do not want to work to get it. The same is true with web copy, so make your copy easy to read. Some tips:

- Write in short paragraphs

- Avoid industry jargon

- Address your visitors directly

- Don't write in passive tense

- Don't repeat yourself

- Get to the point

Visual Impression

No matter how great copy you write, you need to make the page visually appealing. Play around with highlighting, *italics*, **bold text**, CAPS, numbered lists. and bullet points.

Try to break long headlines into a headline and a subheadline. Reduce noise, de-clutter, and add in white space.

If you are completely new to writing, this may seem like a stressful task—I understand that. But just get started writing, and when you are stuck, check out other websites, see how they do it, and get some inspiration.

Getting Started

As with everything in life, it takes practice to master a skill. And the only way to practice is by doing. Just start.

Write some copy, get some feedback from friends and family, and proceed from there.

Oh, and one last thing: **KEEP IT SIMPLE!**

HOW TO GET FREE IMAGES

In the previous section, we talked about the importance of adding visuals to your content.

In recent years, we've seen a rise in the number of websites where stock photos are available for free. I'll clarify what this means before we start to look at these sites.

Some free photographs are entirely free from copyright restrictions, and others are licensed under the Creative Commons public domain license.

What this means is that you can distribute, edit, and use these images however you like without asking permission. However, some images require attributes.

The websites I recommend below don't require permissions. Let's focus on the photos you can download, edit, and use without having to think about anything.

1.   Unsplash

2.   Pexels

3.   StockSnap.io

4.   Pixabay

5.   Picography

Visit these websites, browse through the available content, and see if you can find anything you would like to use on your site.

Just remember to keep it relevant to your website's objectives and your written copy.

CONCLUSION

You now have the toolset to fill up your website with amazing content! I have a lot of respect for you in reaching this stage of the process.

In the next chapter we'll be taking a final look at the website and pushing it live.

CHAPTER 9.
GOING LIVE

Y ou now have a beautiful, unique website with high-converting content. In this section, you will launch it.

You'll learn how to use a professional website checklist, do some last-second tweaking, and make your website accessible to the web by going live!

WEBSITE CHECKLIST

Now is the time to do a final walkthrough of the website. I am going to go through the checklist step by step, so that you can see clearly what we are checking on the website.

We'll start from the top and check off each item as we go.

☐ **Footer Includes Copyright Statement**

Make sure that you have a copyright statement at the bottom of your website in the footer.

It should read something like this: "©2018 [Your Company] Inc."

☐ **Placeholder Images Removed**

Check all the images on your website, ensuring that there are none missing and no placeholder images present.

☐ **Placeholder Text Removed**

Remove all placeholder/dummy text.

Placeholder/dummy text is usually text that you have added for temporary content while you created the site.

It could also have been imported via your theme's demo content.

☐ **Privacy Policy in Place**

With the new General Data Protection Regulation (GDPR) rules, it's important to have a dedicated page for the privacy policy.

It's especially important if you have (or expect to have) visitors from within the European Union.

☐ **Text Free From Spelling Errors**

Proofread every line of text on the website and make sure that the grammar is correct.

☐ **404 Page Existing**

Make sure that you have a "404 Page Not Found" page on your website.

☐ **Descriptive Page Titles**

Every page and every post on your site should have a clear and descriptive title. Check your pages and posts and ensure the titles match the page content.

☐ **Every Page Has Its Unique Title**

Do a check in "Dashboard → Pages' to ensure every page has a unique title. If you find duplicate titles, change them.

☐ **Search Engine Ready**

1. Every page and post should have a unique meta title and meta description (using the Yoast plug-in).

2. Your permalink settings should be set to "Post Name" ("Dashboard → Settings → Permalinks").

3. Your images should have a clear and descriptive title ("Dashboard → Media → Image").

4. Last, but not least, the "Discourage Search Engines from Indexing This Site" checkbox should be unchecked
("Dashboard → Settings → Reading").

☐ **Analytics Tools Installed**

Authenticate MonsterInsights with your Google account, or, if you don't use that plug-in, add the analytics script manually.

(You can copy the analytics script from inside your Google Analytics dashboard. Paste the script within the <head> tags using the customizer.)

☐ **XML Sitemap Is Generated**

Generate an XML sitemap using the Yoast plug-in. You can check if a sitemap is generated by visiting https://yourwebsite.com/sitemap.xml.

☐ **Internal Links Tested**

If you have links within your content that points from one page or post to another, then make sure that they work and point to where they are supposed to.

Broken or irrelevant links make for a bad user experience and can also hurt your SEO.

☐ **External Links Tested**

If you have links within your content that point away from your website, then make sure they work and point to where they are supposed to.

Broken or irrelevant links make for a bad user experience and can also hurt your SEO.

☐   **All Images Use Descriptive Alt Text**

Your images' ALT text can help people (for example, those who use screen-readers) to understand what your images are about.

You should have a descriptive ALT text that explains each image ("Dashboard → Media → Image").

☐   **Forms Display Correctly**

Make sure every contact form and sign-up form displays correctly so that it looks good and makes sense to your visitors.

☐   **Forms Work Correctly**

Make sure every contact form and sign-up form works correctly so that you don't lose important information or the visitors has a bad user experience with forms that don't work.

☐ **Website Is Responsive**

This is a no-brainer nowadays, but you should always double-check to see if every page on your website has great responsiveness.

Check responsiveness by going to "Dashboard → Appearance → Customize" and look at different screen sizes at the bottom of the customizer navigation.

☐ **Browser Compatible**

Test your site on the newer versions of the most popular browsers, like Chrome, Firefox, Internet Explorer, Edge, Safari, and Opera.

☐ **SSL Certificate Added**

The green padlock is a must these days.
Ensure that your website has SSL. If not, contact your hosting provider and get them to help you with that.

☐ **Overall Design Displays Correctly**

Check every inch of your site to see if you spot any irregularities in the design. If you do, fix them before going live.

When you are done going through this checklist, none of the checkboxes should be empty. If something is missing or not working properly, fix it before you proceed.

When you have done so and everything displays correctly, you can pat yourself on the back, because you have done an amazing job!

FINAL TWEAKS

Now that everything is working correctly, close your browser, grab some fresh air and do something completely different for a few hours.

When you feel clearheaded and fit for fight again, visit your website and do a final check-up.

Taking that break and coming back is the best tip I have for you at this stage. It can work wonders for your website because it gives you a fresh perspective, and you will be much more likely to find spelling errors or any other issues that you may have missed earlier when you went through the checklist. Maybe you also want to change something that you didn't notice you didn't like before that break.

So, do your final tweaks now, and when you're done, you are ready to publish your site!

READY TO PUBLISH!

It's unbelievable, right? You have a website that you have created all by yourself, and that is ready to go live!

Now is the time to promote it on social media, tell friends about it, and get it out to the whole world.

You have done an amazing job. Be proud of yourself and continue to explore WordPress. It has endless possibilities, and nothing is stopping you from developing your site even further as you go along.

CHAPTER 10.
YOUR NEXT STEPS

F irst of all, I want to congratulate you! Everyone loves to talk about how they read books, do this, or do that. But very few actually do anything, let alone read a book from start to finish.

You have proven that you have the desire and passion to learn the craft that is WordPress, and this book has been a huge step in what is turning out to be an amazing journey for you.

I would love to be your guide on your path to WordPress glory. And therefore I will keep writing books in order to help you learn everything you need to know.

Remember, the only thing you need to do to get ahead in life is to take action.

So keep up the good work, and I hope we cross paths again in the next book in this series.

ABOUT THE AUTHOR

Dennis Lonmo started his first business in 2008. Since then he has been involved in multiple startups and established businesses in different industries.

Now, a decade later, he is an author and a highly rated online instructor of students hailing from more than 117 countries worldwide.

He runs a consulting business—the very same business that rolled his career into motion all those years ago—as well as a digital agency.

Dennis loves educating and inspiring others to help reach their goals and ambitions in business and in life.

Learn more about Dennis at:

amazon.com/author/dennislonmo

ONE LAST THING

T hank you for taking the time to read this book. I really appreciate it.

If you enjoyed it or found it useful, I would be very grateful if you would post a short review on Amazon.com.

Your support makes a big difference and I personally read all the reviews so that I can make my next book even better.

All you need to do is click the "Review" link on this book's Amazon page.

Thank you for your support!

Dennis Lonmo

RESOURCES

WORDPRESS

WordPress Home
https://wordpress.org/

WordPress Themes
https://wordpress.org/themes/

WordPress Plugins
https://wordpress.org/plugins/

PLUG-INS

Coming Soon Maintenance Mode by SeedProd
https://wordpress.org/plugins/coming-soon/

Sucuri
https://nb.wordpress.org/plugins/sucuri-scanner/

WordFence
https://nn.wordpress.org/plugins/wordfence/

Contact Form 7
https://nb.wordpress.org/plugins/contact-form-7/

MonsterInsights
https://wordpress.org/plugins/google-analytics-for-wordpress/

OptinMonster
https://wordpress.org/plugins/optinmonster/

MailChimp
https://wordpress.org/plugins/mailchimp-for-wp/

UpdraftPlus

https://wordpress.org/plugins/updraftplus/

Yoast SEO
https://nb.wordpress.org/plugins/wordpress-seo/

Envira Gallery
https://wordpress.org/plugins/envira-gallery-lite/

Cloudflare
https://wordpress.org/plugins/cloudflare/

Beaver Builder
https://wordpress.org/plugins/beaver-builder-lite-version/

Ultimate Social Media Icons
https://wordpress.org/plugins/ultimate-social-media-icons/

Easy Google Fonts
https://wordpress.org/plugins/easy-google-fonts/

THEMES

Themeforest
https://themeforest.net/category/wordpress

FONTS

Google Fonts
https://fonts.google.com

FontSquirrel
https://www.fontsquirrel.com

Fonts.com
https://www.fonts.com/

Font Pair
https://fontpair.co/

COLOR SCHEME

Coolors
https://coolors.co/

MARKUP

W3C Markup Validation Tool
https://validator.w3.org/

FREE STOCK PHOTO

Unsplash
https://unsplash.com/

Pexels
https://www.pexels.com/

StockSnap.io
https://stocksnap.io/

Pixabay
https://pixabay.com/

Picography
https://picography.co/

DENNIS LONMO

Website
dennislonmo.com

Amazon Author Profile
amazon.com/author/dennislonmo

Udemy Instructor Profile
https://www.udemy.com/user/dennis-lonmo/

OTHER BOOKS BY DENNIS LONMO

WordPress Like A Boss: A Step-by-Step Guide to Install WordPress Locally and on a Web Host
http://a.co/d/4eQ4EMm